I've got questions

Does God Take Naps?

written by Crystal Bowman and Teri McKinley | illustrated by Ailie Busby

TYNDALE KIDS

Tyndale House Publishers, Inc.
Carol Stream, IL

Visit Tyndale's website for kids at www.tyndale.com/kids.

TYNDALE is a registered trademark of Tyndale House Publishers, Inc. The Tyndale Kids logo is a trademark of Tyndale House Publishers, Inc.

Does God Take Naps?

Designed by Jacqueline L. Nuñez

Edited by Sarah Rubio

Scripture quotations are taken from the *Holy Bible*, New Living Translation, copyright © 1996, 2004, 2015 by Tyndale House Foundation. Used by permission of Tyndale House Publishers, Inc., Carol Stream, Illinois 60188. All rights reserved.

For manufacturing information regarding this product, please call 1-800-323-9400.

For information about special discounts for bulk purchases, please contact Tyndale House Publishers at csresponse@tyndale.com or call 800-323-9400.

Library of Congress Cataloging-in-Publication Data
Names: Bowman, Crystal, author.
Title: Does God take naps? / written by Crystal Bowman and Teri McKinley.
Description: Carol Stream, IL : Tyndale House Publishers, Inc., 2017. |
    Series: I've got questions
Identifiers: LCCN 2016015563 | ISBN 9781496417411 (hc)
Subjects: LCSH: God (Christianity)--Juvenile literature.
Classification: LCC BT107 .B68 2017 | DDC 231--dc23 LC record available at https://lccn.loc.gov/2016015563

Printed in China

23	22	21	20	19	18	17
7	6	5	4	3	2	1

In loving memory of Dana,
who shared Christ's love through her care and love for children.

LORD, there is no one like you!
For you are great, and your name is full of power.

Jeremiah 10:6

Kids have lots of questions!
Do you have questions too—
of who God is and what he does
and how he cares for you?

2

Let's talk about those questions,
so you can learn and grow.
Get ready for some awesome things
that God wants you to know.

I know that God's important,
but can you tell me why?
Does God have superpowers?
Is he bigger than the sky?

God created everyone.
He put the stars in space.
He's ruler of the universe
and keeps the world in place.

4

I know that God's in heaven;
I wonder where that is.
Does he own a great big mansion?
Can I have a house like his?

God has a great big mansion
that's as pretty as can be!
And someday we will live with him;
there's room for you and me.

Does God take naps like I do?
Does he travel far away?
Does he sleep when he is tired
from a very busy day?

The Bible says God
never sleeps.
He watches his creation.
He doesn't need to
take a nap
or go on a vacation.

9

Can I really talk to God?
I know he's everywhere.
But does he ever talk to me,
and does he hear my prayer?

God's words are in the Bible.
He talks to you that way.
And every time you talk to God,
he hears the words you say.

11

I want to make God smile.
I want to make him glad.
What can I do to please him,
so God will not be sad?

The Bible says God loves us,
and God wants your love too.
Thank him for the gifts he gives;
be kind in all you do.

12

13

Does God have pets, like dogs or cats?
I think he might have four.
But maybe he has ten or twelve,
or maybe even more.

God owns all the animals.
He watches as they sleep.
He helps the robins build
    their nests
and feeds the hungry sheep.

14

15

I think that God is very old.
I know he's still alive.
I wonder just how old he is.
My guess is forty-five.

God has always been alive;
he's not like you and me.
I know it's hard to
    understand,
but God will always be.

16

Does God see when I'm crying
and when I'm sad inside?
Does he know when I am scared
or want to run and hide?

God cares about your
    problems.
He sees each of your tears.
His love will help and
    comfort you
and take away your fears.

18

19

Does God like eating pizza
or maybe mac and cheese?
Does God eat all his vegetables,
like brussels sprouts and peas?

God doesn't need to
eat or drink
or cook food like we do.
But he created
vegetables
and sweet treats just
for you.

20

21

How does God keep learning?
And why is he so smart?
Does God like pretty colors?
Is he very good at art?

Everything there is to know,
God already knows.
He paints the evening sunsets
and colors every rose.

22

23

Does God have any children?
Does God have girls and boys?
Does he ever give them presents
and let them play with toys?

Jesus is the Son of God,
and you're God's child too.
All the things that you
enjoy
are gifts God gives to you.

24

I know that God's a loving King
who's ruling over me.
But does he sit upon a throne
like other royalty?

God tells us in the Bible
that heaven is his throne.
God's the greatest King of all;
we worship him alone.

God wants you to understand
that he is everywhere.
He watches you all day and night
and keeps you in his care.

He gives his children happiness
and blessings from above.
And nothing in the whole wide world
is greater than his love.

29

More books by
Crystal Bowman and Teri McKinley

My Mama & Me
Rhyming Devotions for You and Your Child
written by Crystal Bowman & Teri McKinley
ISBN 978-1-4143-7973-9

M is for Manger
written by Crystal Bowman & Teri McKinley
pictures by Claire Keay
ISBN 978-1-4964-2004-6

The One Year DEVOTIONS for Preschoolers
illustrated by Elena Kucharik
little Blessings
ISBN 978-0-8423-8940-2

I've got questions
Do Baby Bears Have Mommies?
written by Crystal Bowman and Teri McKinley | illustrated by Ailie Busby
ISBN 978-1-4964-1740-4

I've got questions
Does God Take Naps?
written by Crystal Bowman and Teri McKinley | illustrated by Ailie Busby
ISBN 978-1-4964-1741-1

Purchase these books online or at your favorite retailer.

CP1236